Greater Than a T Plymouth Massachusetts USA

50 Travel Tips from a Local

Samantha Anderson

Order Information: To order this title please email lbrenenc@gmail.com or visit GreaterThanATourist.com. A bulk discount can be provided.

Cover Template Creator: Lisa Rusczyk Ed. D. using Canva.
Cover Creator: Lisa Rusczyk Ed. D.
Image: https://pixabay.com/en/lighthouse-sea-red-white-port-2275312/

Lock Haven, PA
ISBN: 9781549776939

TABLE OF CONTENTS

DEDICATION

This book is dedicated to the amazing people of Plymouth, who take pride in our beautiful, historic town and do their best to keep it going. Also, to my Nana. Thank you for inspiring me to write and to find the beauty in everything. I love you, you are my sunshine!

Samantha Anderson

FROM THE PUBLISHER

Traveling can be one of the most important parts of a person's life. The anticipation and memories that you have are some of the best. As a publisher of the Greater Than a Tourist book series, as well as the popular 50 Things to Know book series, we strive to help you learn about new places, spark your imagination, and inspire you. Wherever you are and whatever you do I wish you safe, fun, and inspiring travel.

Lisa Rusczyk Ed. D.

CZYK Publishing

Samantha Anderson

1. When in Plymouth, You Must Visit Plimoth Plantation

Plimoth Plantation is one of the biggest tourist attractions that Plymouth has to offer. Not only is Plimoth Plantation a tourist attraction, but it is also a top field trip spot for the local schools. The Plantation offers a look into Pilgrim life. See how the Pilgrims lived once they landed in Plymouth and built up their colony. There is so much to learn at Plimoth Plantation. For example, did you know that the Mayflower first landed at Provincetown? The Pilgrims did not make it to Plymouth until a month after they hit the new land. Fun fact: Plymouth was spelled as Plimoth by the Pilgrims, which is why the spelling is "incorrectly" for the attraction.

At Plimoth Plantation, everything is set back in time. The huts are replicas of what you would see going down the streets of Plymouth in the 1620's, the wardrobe is exactly what the Pilgrims would have worn, no matter what the season was, and the knowledge and vocabulary align with the times. You can try to stump the actors by asking them to take a selfie with you or asking what a Snapchat is, but you may get accused of witchcraft!

Don't forget to visit the Wampanoag tribe at Plimoth Plantation. They represent the natives that helped the Pilgrims survive in the new land. These Native Americans are often crafting something to align with their culture while being played by actual Native Americans. This cannot be missed.

7. The Jenney Grist Mill is a Hidden Gem

While residents of Plymouth all know about the Jenney Grist Mill, it is hidden in plain sight to our tourist friends. The Jenney Grist Mill, also called The Plimoth Grist Mill, is a working mill. The Plimoth Grist Mill is ultimately the reproduction of the Jenney Grist Mill, but the same concept and structure are in place. This mill was used for grinding corn. Originally named for its owner, John Jenney, this mill was the first of the town. It is also one of the many ways Mr. Jenney could feed his family.

How does this mill work? It runs on water power, turning corn into cornmeal. Visiting the mill, you get a full tour of the grist mill and get to learn all the ins and outs about how it works. You will always want to call the store in advance to make sure that they are doing the corn milling the day you plan to visit, as they do not do this daily. This is a great attraction, especially if you like to know how machinery works.

After you see how everything works, you will absolutely want to shop the Plimoth Grist Mill store. There is cornmeal, fresh from the mill, as well as other fun goodies. You may even be able to get a book or Plymouth souvenir without all of the crowding of the stores that are right on the waterfront. This will not take you a full day, so plan it for a lowkey day or when you have other activities you would like to do. There is also a pizza place right around the corner if you get hungry.

8. Find Out If You Are a Part of All of This By Visiting the Mayflower Society House

Attention ancestry buffs! Have you always wanted to know how your family got to the United States? Do you want to be able to confirm that your ancestors came over on the Mayflower? Look no further than the Mayflower Society House.

Not just anyone can join the General Society of Mayflower Descendants. While anyone is welcome to tour, you must be able to prove your lineage to a Mayflower passenger in order to join. Ideally, if you have a family member that is a member of the society, you can use whatever they used as documentation. If not, you will have to hunt down some paperwork from at least one Pilgrim to prove your ancestry. Once you are in though, you get to be a part of some really interesting events and meetings. It feels like a bit of an exclusive club.

You can also tour this beautiful, historic house for a small fee. While many people associate Plymouth only with the Pilgrims, this house was also an important part of the Revolutionary Era and World War II. This house is not handicap accessible and will not be made to be so due to its historic nature.

9. Lobster Tales and Pirate Cruises Are Fun for All Ages

Downtown Plymouth is right on the ocean. One of the perks behind this is that there are boats that go out for days of fun and adventure through Plymouth Harbor. Plymouth Cruises hosts both the Lobster Tales cruises and the Pirate Cruises. There is so much fun to be had, even for the little ones!

On Lobster Tales, you can become a lobster harvester! You will be provided with the opportunity to learn about lobster traps, lobsters, and other marine life that you may happen to catch. Will you capture a rare lobster during your travels? Some lucky individuals get to help band the claws, pull up the traps, and more. Be sure to bring your camera for any potential photo opportunities.

Pirate Cruises are a blast. Here, you are submerged in

the adventure. Everyone is a pirate. Your mission is to go get your treasure back from enemy pirates. Water cannons are involved! Everyone on this cruise gets a pirate hat, some treasure, and other pirate goodies. Similar to the Lobster Tales, you will find some treasure within lobster traps as well! This makes for a fun day on the water!

Bonus for the adults: if you get a chance to break away from the kids, there are also wine tasting cruises available from Plymouth Cruises. Talk about relaxing! Not only do you get to enjoy some wine and food, but you also get to learn a little bit about all of the wines that are being offered. Impress your friends at your next dinner party.

10. Captain John Boats Are a Well-Known Staple to the Town

Captain John Boats are a huge part of the fun of Plymouth. They sail out of the same harbor as Plymouth Cruises. They may even be docked next to each other. Captain John offers a variety of services including whale watches, deep sea fishing, and trips around the harbor. There is something for everyone that loves the sea.

Going on a whale watch with Captain John is a true Plymouth highlight. Right now, Plymouth has experienced an increased amount of Great White Shark sightings, so you may even be able to see one of these amazing creatures. How many whales do you think you will see? The amount varies and is purely based on luck. But, when you get up close and personal with a whale, it is absolutely breathtaking. This goes without saying, but if you get seasick, this excursion is not

31

for you. The ship bathrooms are small and uncomfortable for those that do not do well with waves, so do not try to tough it out!

Deep sea fishing is a very popular attraction. There are often competitions within groups of people that go to see who will catch the largest fish. It is a day made to relax while entertaining you simultaneously. You can even buy the fish you catch to bring home for dinner. This is not for you if you are queasy, as they will clean the fish on the ship, but being able to say you caught and brought dinner home is always a good feeling. Bonus: you may see whales or sharks on this trip, too. It all depends on your luck.

"Being thus arrived in a good harbor, and brought to safe land, they fell upon their knees and blessed the God of Heaven who had brought them over the vast and furious ocean, and delivered them from all the perils and miseries thereof, again to set their feet on the firm and stable earth, their proper element" - *William Bradford about landing in Plymouth*

Samantha Anderson

11. Ice Cream Makes Everything Better

It is not often that you come across someone that can resist one of Plymouth's ice cream shops. While these shops are primarily seasonal, based on the summer tourist season, you will not be disappointed by waiting in line to get ice cream. There are three places that I will always recommend: Pebbles, Ziggy's, and Peaceful Meadows.

Pebbles is located right across from where the Mayflower II is normally docked (the Mayflower II gift shops remain intact while the ship is gone, so look for those). This is one of the iconic waterfront shops that you must visit. It is entirely outdoors, although there is an awning that shelters those that can grab a seat from the sun or even the rain. While they serve more than ice cream, including incredibly delicious fries, who doesn't love jumping to dessert?

Ziggy's has the most delicious lime sherbet around. It is

always super busy, but when you taste it, you will see why. There is a walk-up window for those that exclusively want ice cream, but you can go inside of the tiny shop to order food, or if you would prefer to order your ice cream in there. It is located right across from the harbor, so once you get your ice cream, walk across the street and sit on one of the benches. At sunset, the views are breathtaking. Ice cream with a view!

Peaceful Meadows is a personal and all-around favorite. Their flavors are fun, their prices are right, and the employees are friendly. All their ice cream is homemade and you can taste that difference. It is a local mini-chain that you cannot pass up. From their shakes to their sundaes, everything is delicious. It is even away from a little bit of the craziness that can occur downtown, so it is a great break.

12. Have Your Cupcake and Eat It, Too

I could rant and rave about our fantastic dessert places for days. There are three major bakeries that I think of when I want a cupcake or something sweet. They are: Guilty Bakery, Piece of Cake, and Cupcake Charlie's.

Guilty Bakery is a small bakery with big potential. They design cakes, cupcakes, and other sweets for all different types of events. Their design work is incredible and their flavor profiles are out of this world. If you can stop in to this bakery, grab a box of treats and be sure to get some French macarons. On the weekends, if you get their early enough, they have freshly baked donuts as well. They are going to go far in Plymouth despite being relatively new to the scene.

Piece of Cake has been around for a bit in Plymouth. They have some of the absolute best chocolate cake in the town. They also make cakes and other goodies for all different types of events. If you stop into the store, you can

37

pick up some cookies or cupcakes. Make sure you get some chocolate cake, not matter what. It is a piece of heaven.

Cupcake Charlie's is a chain cupcake store primarily based in Massachusetts. The owner was even on Food Network's *Cupcake Wars.* They offer up some yummy cupcakes with super sweet frosting for anyone with a killer sweet tooth. Each day, they offer a new flavor of the day, with some of my personal favorites normally happening in the fall. They have the most adorable little shop that reminds me a bit of the 1950s. Grab a cupcake and surround yourself with the smell of sweet frosting. Enjoy! The only downside is that parking can be impossible to find, especially in the summer. You may have to park by Nelson Street Beach and walk down.

13. Higher End Restaurants Can Be Found On the Water

If you are looking for a nice, romantic night out, stay close to the water. The restaurants that have the most romantic vibe can be found down that strip. These restaurants have views of the ocean, seasonal outdoor seating, and some incredible food.

A staple to downtown, and my personal favorite, is Isaac's. Isaac's is named for an outcast of the Pilgrims, Isaac Allerton. But this restaurant is no outcast. The food is delicious with local seafood being served up regularly. A few favorites include their chicken and broccoli penne as well as their Fisherman's Platter, which is a special that they offer from time to time. It is a little on the pricy side, but it worth every penny. If you are given the option to get a side dish, request the butternut squash with some cheese. It sounds bizarre, but it is amazing. Parking can be tough to come by, but a lot of people do not realize that there is a valet lot behind the restaurant. Do not forget to tip your valet!

About two doors down is Mamma Mia's. This is a Plymouth favorite for everything. You can order a fancy pasta dish or a simple pizza and will almost always be impressed. They have a fabulous catering menu as well, should you have to plan the food for a function while you are in town. Do not pass up a chance to go here, even if you decide to opt for the more casual side.

A little way down the street is East Bay Grille. They have an extensive menu of various seafood entrees as well as some other carnivorous plates, such as the Colossal Lobster Tail or the Town Wharf Sirloin. Their appetizers are just as delicious and as filling as some of their entrees. Be sure to visit with an empty stomach and a full wallet. This restaurant is right on the water and if you get the chance to sit outside, you could see some beautiful sights.

14. Main Street and Court Street Are for Nightlife

If you are looking for a night out on the town with some friends, you will want to head out to Main Street and Court Street. These streets are where the restaurants and bars with the most fun reputations (and latest hours) are. If there is something that Plymouth is abundant in, it is bars.

To list them all would take another entire guide, so I would recommend bar hopping until you find the fit for you. There are some hidden gems that are advertisements for not judging a book by its cover, such as Driftwood Tavern, a small restaurant with an amazing, unique menu. Most of our bars feature live, local bands Thursday through Sunday for your listening pleasure.

If you are a sports fan, Main Street Bar and Grill is great all season around. Just be wary if you are promoting that you are not a Boston fan, especially during playoff season. Rivalries and alcohol do not mix.

One of the popular places for the locals is Sam Diego's. Most of the college students reunite here when they come home for breaks. During the day, it is a great family restaurant. But at night, this Tex-Mex restaurant is a huge hit, serving up great drinks and munchies.

T-Bones is great if you enjoy a country-like atmosphere. They offer line dancing a few nights out of the week with some instruction as well. Grab your boots and dance your way downtown!

15. Local Breweries and Distilleries Offer Fun for Adults

Plymouth seems to have breweries and distilleries popping up all over the place. Not only is this great for all of our local restaurants, but this is wonderful for tourism. Tasting a locations alcohol really gives you a glimpse into the town.

Dirty Water Distillery is a family business right by the waterfront. They are a micro-distillery that makes artisanal liquor. They have fun names for some of their products, such as Sue-E Bacon Vodka and Bogmonster Cranberry Gin. This business takes pride on experimenting with different flavor combinations to bring a unique taste to Plymouth. You can walk right in while they are open, try some samples for a small donation, and even buy some alcohol or merchandise. Plymouth is huge in supporting local businesses, so join us!

We also are home to Mayflower Brewery, a microbrewery. They have been open for about a decade in Plymouth, but they are really jumping off now. There are flavors that they offer year-round and flavors based on things that are unique to New England, such as the weather and the celebrations. Here, you can tour the brewery or do a tasting. Why not do both? Maybe if enough people go, they will name something after this book! Worth a shot, right?

16. Breakfast is One of Our Best Meals

While all of the food in Plymouth is good, breakfast is absolutely huge. For some reason, it is one of the busiest meals that I have encountered in all of my time here. There is one place that does breakfast better than all of the rest- Water Street Café.

Water Street Café is located on the corner of Water Street. It is not a flashy building, just a very simple, small restaurant. While it may be small, the food is incredible. If you are going on a weekend day, you either want to get their as soon as they open or closer to a "brunch" time, or else you may have quite the wait in front of you.

Their crunchy French toast and home fries are out of this world. If you really want to get the best of everything, you'll get the sampler. You will not leave Water Street hungry. The prices are modest and the service is great. Their coffee is even good, which is a huge bonus.

If you are mobility impaired, you will have to use the back entrance, as the front has very steep stairs. There is not really much parking in the back since there are apartments, but try to find a spot if you need to use the ramp. If not, parking is located next door in a full gravel parking lot. It can get tight in there and sometimes people get creative with their parking. But your first bite of home fries will tell you why.

17. Souvenir Shops Galore- The Best Places to Buy Your Plymouth Garb

On Water Street, you will find a strip of little shops that house all of our souvenirs. There are three shops that are on that strip with another on Main Street. Every gift shop offers similar things in terms of modern day merchandise, but the little shops next to the Mayflower II's dock offer some fun Pilgrim related merchandise. If you collect certain types of souvenirs, like spoons or thimbles, consider checking these shops first.

Earlier in this book, I mentioned Pebbles Ice Cream. If you leave that restaurant and continue towards the Captain John Boats, you will pass the gift shops with modern merchandise. This is where you can get your Plymouth sweatshirts, pun filled t-shirts, and other souvenirs that can help you remember your time in Plymouth fondly. While I am unsure if this is common in other tourist locations, you will see a lot of locals wearing sweatshirts that say Plymouth or Boston on them. Although we are about an hour out from Boston, you will hear anyone in our area say they are from Boston. Whether or not this is some kind of pride related to our sports teams or to our history is a mystery to me, but almost everyone owns at least one thing with Plymouth or Boston on it. Buying and wearing your Plymouth merchandise will not make you look like a tourist, it will actually make you look like a local!

18. The Waterfront Festival- A Great Way to Sample Plymouth

If you are coming to town the last weekend of August, you are in luck! That is when Plymouth tends to host its annual Waterfront Festival. This is a major event in Plymouth that is fun for all ages. All of Water Street gets closed down to allow vendors and entertainers to come down for a day of supporting locals.

One of the most notable parts of this day would be the duck race. During the day, you can purchase rubber duckies to race on your behalf down the stream. Each duck is numbered are released into the stream with all of the other ducks. The winner gets a prize. For years, kids and kids at heart have been participating in this, even dressing up as ducks as good luck prior to their release. It is great fun and acts as a fundraiser for Plymouth.

There are so many vendors at these events that you will not want to leave your wallet at home. Some of these vendors make everything with local materials, some make products that pay homage to Plymouth, and others have businesses based within the area. No matter which way you look at it, you are supporting Plymouth's economy by shopping from these little pop up tents. There are all sorts of goods and services being sold, from dog accessories to local honey.

The food tends to be local as well. With food trucks being a hot trend this decade, they have been prevalent during the last couple festivals. There are also stands hosted by local restaurants and chefs aiming to spread their business. No matter what, you will find something delicious. Grab a bag of kettle corn before you leave.

19. Pedi-Cabs, Because We Do Not Have Many Ubers

In a time where Uber and Lyft are in their prime, Plymouth has a considerably low number of drivers for these services. In this element, we are still back in 1620. Taxis can be expensive. What is the best way to get around downtown Plymouth? Pedi-cabs.

If you are unfamiliar with pedi-cabs, essentially consider it as a small horse drawn carriage with a person instead of a horse. The people are driving bicycles with carts attached to the back. These are great if there are only a couple of you, but are not ideal for large families.

It may not be as romantic as a horse drawn carriage, but it is an efficient, cruelty-free way of getting around the chaos that can develop in downtown Plymouth. These people are incredibly hard-working and always very pleasant. Pedi-cabs are considered to be highly innovative and environmentally

51

friendly as well. You may not get a chance to experience a pedi-cab again, so why not take a ride? Even if it is just to bring you from one of the ice cream shops down to a cupcake shop, it is worth it for the experience alone. Enjoy the wind in your hair and the smell of the ocean while you get carted downtown.

20. Plymouth Memorial Hall is Great for Cage Fights

Plymouth Memorial Hall is both a building to pay tribute to veterans and an entertainment venue. On the main floor, just through the doors, is the hall of remembrance. This is one area that will always remain untouched during events. There are uniforms of soldiers, tribute videos being played, and other items and displays honoring our veterans. On the other floors, you will find the event and entertainment spaces.

This venue can host about 1600 people seated in their main room. The number one attraction here tends to be cage fights or MMA fights. People come from all around to see these fights. These are the events that sell out. But these are not the only events you can find here. This is a fantastic concert venue and has hosted comedy concerts as charity events. It is always a great idea to check their event calendar before coming into town to see if there is anything that you can see while you are here.

If you are coming here to do a destination wedding or to host another function, Memorial Hall is a great place for that as well. The hall manager will work with you to make the function you want to plan one for the books. Memorial Hall can be completely transformed with just a little bit of uplighting and some decorations. Check out their website for more pictures.

"The pilgrims on the Mayflower landed at Plymouth Rock. To my knowledge, they didn't wait around for a return trip to Europe. You settle some place with a purpose. If you don't want to do that, stay home. You avoid an awful lot of risks by not venturing outward"

-Buzz Aldrin

Samantha Anderson

21. Village Landing Is Hidden In Plain Sight

While venturing around downtown Plymouth, you will see tons of little shops. When you get towards the end of the strip, a little way before Nelson Street, there are a couple restaurants that you can see from the road in a place called Village Landing. There is so much more to Village Landing than what you can see from the street.

There is not much parking in the back, so you may have to walk a bit. But when you get there, you will find some of the places I have referenced before, such as Peaceful Meadows and Piece of Cake. There are also quite a few boutique shops that you can get some beautiful jewelry or fun accessories from. There are a lot of beachy themed stores within this area. As you go deeper into the area, you will find quite a few restaurants that you can try out. Their food always smells delicious. A very well-known chocolate shop calls Village Landing home- Fedele's. Their fudge is too good to be true.

There are quite a few picnic tables outside to sit and enjoy any of the food you get from the little shops, or if you just need a little break. There are even some mini-rides for the kids that you can use a quarter or two to make it work. Do not miss out on these shops, restaurants, and fun places just because it is off the beaten path by a hair!

22. Why Are There So Many Lobsters?

Walking and driving around Plymouth, you will likely encounter a few five-foot lobster statues. This is a fun activity for you to participate in, no matter what age you are. The activity is the Plymouth Lobster Crawl. These lobsters are placed all over downtown Plymouth. Will you be able to find them all?

Each lobster was sponsored by a local business and was designed by a local artist. Each lobster reflects something different. Most of the lobsters reflect the business that sponsored them, but some of them are just decorated in fun. The Plymouth Area Chamber of Commerce started this as a tourist attraction, but as a local, I love to try to spot ones I have not seen before while I am downtown.

You can get a map of the lobster locations on the Plymouth Chamber of Commerce website. Find all 29!

23. Free Fun at Nelson Street Beach

Nelson Street Beach has been a location for fun for years. Since I was young, I have been going there to watch the fireworks on the Fourth of July. Now, Nelson Street is even more fun for children and for beach goers alike.

There are two different playground sets at Nelson Street Beach. One is for the littler kids that may be intimidated by the older kids or by the size of the older kid slides. The other is for older kids that are a little more fearless. These playsets can provide hours of fun. They are located on the field part of Nelson Street Beach, so you can also bring frisbees and balls and play in the field if the kids get tired of the playset. There is also a splash pad for the kids to run and play around in, especially on the warmer days. Do not worry, no one will tell if you run through to cool down as well.

There is also a beautiful beach to walk right at this park. It is right next to the playground. Sometimes, it can be a little rocky, so I would recommend water shoes or something else on your feet. This is a great place to watch the sunset and to get pictures if you are a photographer.

There is a cute little snack stand at the entrance. This is a seasonal little restaurant where you can grab things like burgers and hot dogs to feed yourself and the kids during a full day of play. You can also pack your own picnic lunch.

If you feel like running or walking, there is a walk path that starts in the parking lot of Nelson Street Beach. There are a lot of people that walk their dogs down this path, so Rover is welcome!

24. Bond With the Family Over This Daring Outdoor Activity

If you and your family tend to be daring, DropZone may be the perfect place for you. Several members of my family have gone and loved it, but I am not the most daring person around. If you plan on going here, plan on spending most of the day embracing your inner daredevil.

What can you find at DropZone? There are parallel zip lines for you to race your friend or sibling on. Who will reach the end first? Just hold on tight! There is also a high ropes obstacle course. What is this? Just an obstacle course that is far off the ground that requires a lot of concentration and, in some case, teamwork. This is a great way to test your limits. DropZone does focus on safety and there are helmets and harnesses for everyone. If you are looking for a thrill, but all of that is a little too fast for you, there is a climbing/rock wall that you can test yourself on to see how high you can make it up. Of course, if your anxiety gets too high, you can take up mini golf for a day.

DropZone is open in the autumn and the summer and they recommend making a reservation if you have a larger group. Look them up online to see what their hours are when you come to visit.

25. Rainy Day? This Local Business Is A Must for the Creative and Want to Be Creatives

Claychick is one of the best local businesses around in terms of community involvement, fun, and entertainment. Located away from Plymouth center, Claychick is a paint-your-own pottery shop. All of the employees are incredibly passionate about this. Owner, Chickie, will tell you that this is fun art, not fine art. Even if you think you are a terrible artist, there is something that you can do here and it will come out gorgeous.

Claychick has a great selection of items to paint. From figurines of princesses and other kid's pop culture figures, dinnerware for the adults, and miscellaneous fun items. The employees will walk you through every step of the process. If you want to use a stamp or stencil to make your design complete, they will help you learn how to properly use it and will guide you as you complete your art.

In most cases, the item has to be fired at Claychick to be finished, which takes about a week. However, you can talk to the owner to see if a local pottery place near you can fire this to have the same outcome. Chickie and the Claychicks will help you figure out a way to make this work.

You will spend a lot of time here perfecting your art. I have personally spent over six hours glazing a piece of pottery before. You set your own speed. It is fun even when the sun is shining bright. Embrace your inner artist.

26. Brewster Gardens is Beautifully Picturesque

There is a beautiful garden at the beginning of Water Street called Brewster Gardens. It recently went through a bunch of renovations to make it even more striking. There are statues that pay homage to some of the town's best, a beautiful stream (where the duck race is held), and of course tons of flowers and greenery around.

Consider taking a stroll through this beautiful area. There are pathways through the entire garden. Cross over the stream on our new gorgeous foot bridge and take a look at some of the fish in the stream. As you walk further up, you can go through a couple small tunnels. If you walk far enough, you will end up at the Jenney Grist Mill. Not many tourists know that you can walk to there from Water Street, so that is a pro insider tip!

If you are planning something, like a proposal or a family photo shoot, this is the place to do it. You will end up with gorgeous pictures no matter what the weather is and what part you are in. As a matter of fact, it started raining on my wedding day and my pictures were at Brewster Gardens. They ended up being gorgeous. Granted, I credit my photographer for that, but the scenery definitely added to the beauty. I took someone's engagement pictures there one evening and it was extremely dark, but the pictures were stunning. Photographers, both professional and recreational, this is a great spot for all sorts of pictures. Plus, there is no admission fee!

27. Plymouth Extends Beyond Downtown

When most people think of Plymouth, they think of Downtown Plymouth. That is a common occurrence in every tourist destination, but particularly here. But if you are on our main highway, which is named Pilgrim Highway, Plymouth extends from exit 2 through 7. Our town is huge!

Each area of Plymouth has different villages. There is Manomet, Cedarville, and Chiltonville to name a few. But then Plymouth is divided into north, south, and west Plymouth. That is right, no one refers to east Plymouth.

Venture off away from downtown. There is so much to see in Plymouth and so many local businesses to explore. Support the areas that do not necessarily get all of the tourists during tourist season. You can get to a beach from any of the exits, so if you are coming in the summer and want to avoid Cape Cod traffic, get off the highway and take some of the back roads. There are also tons of local restaurants, shops, and even landmarks through the entire town. A lot of people miss out by only sticking to downtown!

28. The Sheriff's Farm Has Beautiful Plants and a Petting Zoo

Off of exit 5, the Sheriff's Department runs a few greenhouses and a petting zoo. Here, you can get the most beautiful seasonal flowers. We go every year just to get the mums to decorate our front porch for fall.

The prices are incredibly modest. You go in, look through the greenhouses and other plant areas for what you are looking for, and then bring everything to the front on a little trolley. If you need help, the Sheriff's Department employs inmates from the local prison to work the area. Do not be nervous, there are plenty of officers around if you are skittish.

The pumpkins that the Sheriff's Department sells are always the perfect pumpkins for decorating or for carving. There is a great variety of sizes, from tiny gourds to hearty pumpkins. It will fulfill your fall needs. Brighten up where you are staying with some flowers and pumpkins. This is particularly great if you have kids and are traveling around Halloween. No one has to miss out on the festivities!

29. Bringing Fido? We Are Building a Dog Park

Friends of Plymouth Dog Park is currently in the fundraising stages, but it is something that locals are particularly excited about. There are constantly fundraisers going on to help fund this park. Why is it needed? Almost one out of six people in Plymouth own a dog. With tourists bringing their dogs into Plymouth when they travel, there is even more of a need for this park.

While we do not know when it is opening yet, you can help support the building of this park, especially if you intend on making Plymouth one of your regular vacation spots. You can check their website to see if there is a fundraising event when you come to town so you can support all of the pups of Plymouth!

There are also occasional meet ups for dogs at local parks. Check out some Plymouth pages on social media sites to see if there is one happening when you are here and to see if you need to register. Not only will your dog have a great time, but you will get to socialize with the dog lovers of Plymouth and enjoy quality time with your own dog. That is a win-win situation!

Samantha Anderson

30. The Farmer's Market

Our Farmer's Market is like no other. You can find some of the yummiest, freshest food here, even for the pickiest eater. The Farmer's Market is currently seasonal, from June through October, but that could change. Like most of Plymouth's events and destinations, there is something for everyone.

Whether you want some fresh fruits and vegetables for your stay here, or you want some baked goods to munch on, you are in luck! Even our gluten-free friends have a wonderful option for baked goods here with a local company serving up everything from gluten free breads to pies!

What is better than fresh food? Fresh food and music! The Farmer's Market features local musicians as entertainment while the market is open. How fun is that? If you are there on the right day, there may even be some local businesses selling items like soaps, candles, and pet supplies.

74

Currently, the market is open on Thursday's, but be sure to check the website to see if that changes by the time you come visit.

Samantha Anderson

"Put this another way: she was only about twelve feet longer than a tennis court. And she had been designed not as a passenger ship, but for cargo." –

Kevin Jackson, <u>Mayflower: The Voyage from Hell</u>

Samantha Anderson

31. Our High Schools Act As Businesses with Cheap Services

Plymouth is home to two high schools- North and South. While there is an extreme rivalry between the schools, they both prepare students for the real world. Plymouth South is the main technical high school, while also offering regular academic programs. Plymouth North recently added a few more technical studies to their school.

Both high schools have been completely rebuilt within the past few years, with Plymouth South finishing right before the 2017 school year began. What services can you find offered at South? The three that people frequent the most include culinary, cosmetology, and automotive. At culinary, you can grab a bite to eat and get desserts for a great price. In the cosmetology program, you can get you hair and nails done for a fraction of the price while the students get their hours in to become certified cosmetologists. Automotive will help you with any of your car issues, from tire changes to oil changes. Each of the technical programs, which extends beyond the three listed, is taught by experts in the field. There is real life experience in the classroom constantly. These students graduate with a regular diploma and a certificate in their program. It is incredible for the futures of all of these students.

32. Close to "Bean"town- Coffee Fixes Are Everywhere

While the "bean" in Beantown refers to baked beans, people from Massachusetts love their coffee. Like most places, we have the usual coffee shops like Starbucks and Dunkin Donuts (a Massachusetts staple), but our local coffee shops are even better.

Jolly Bean Café is one of our newer coffee shops, but it has taken Plymouth by storm. Fun fact: the owner, Amanda, started this coffee shop in the lobby of Plymouth's DMV! Now, she is in her own shop and has amazing food and drinks served up daily, except for Sundays. You can stop here to get your morning coffee and muffin, or you can come here for an afternoon pick me up and lunch. Jolly Bean has a special blend of coffee made just for their store. They have seasonal drinks that put the traditional PSL to shame, with

Pumpkin Pie being your new fall obsession. My personal favorite combination involves chocolate and coconut within my iced coffee. If you go, tell her that Sammie sent you.

Another huge hit is Marylou's. Marylou's is great for specialty flavored drinks. The pink and black color scheme will capture your attention first, but then you will taste your first coffee and be pulled in. From Girl Scout Cookie to Oreo Cookie Monster, there are plenty of combinations to try. I would recommend the Mochanillanut iced coffee for those with a sweet tooth.

33. Hotels and B&B's To Use

Plymouth has hotels and bed and breakfasts all throughout the town. Most people like to stay close to the waterfront, as they expect that they will be spending most of their time there. Often times, the hotels close to main attractions will be more costly than the ones on other exits. That can also depend on the season.

The three places I would recommend that are on the waterfront, or are within walking distance, are Hotel 1620, The John Carver Inn, and the Seabreeze Bed and Breakfast. These hotels all come with great recommendations from locals that have had their families stay there in the past, or that have stayed there for a Staycation. The John Carver Inn has been around the longest of the three and offers a fun, themed indoor waterpark within it. These three hotels fill up quickly around tourist time, so be sure to book in advance if you are coming during a popular time.

Other than those locations, there are plenty of other options. If you want to be close to downtown, but not in the middle of all of the festivities, consider looking at hotels right off exit 5. If all Plymouth hotels appear to be full, but you are set on coming, consider looking for hotels in one of the following towns: Kingston, Carver, and Bourne.

34. White Horse Beach- Catch Rays and Meet Celebrities

White Horse Beach is one of the most popular beaches in Plymouth. You will want to avoid it on July 3, as the locals have made their own holiday, but other than that it is fair game. This beach is located in Manomet, a village of Plymouth.

This beach has gorgeous views. You can often spot seals in the distance while you sunbathe, build sandcastles, or play in the water. Remember, seals are the number one food group for sharks, so do not try to get close to the seals by walking towards them or kayaking towards them. Plymouth made headlines everywhere one year for a kayaker having a shark bite their kayak. There is a little general store a walk away from the beach, but I would recommend packing a cooler. This way, you will not lose your sandy spot on the beach.

Plymouth has experienced an increase in celebrity sightings lately. I, personally, do not go up to celebrities. I will admit that it is purely because I am star struck, but they are also just people. However, some of our frequent visitors include members of New Kids on the Block, Mark Wahlberg, and Brett Michaels among others. It is always fun to see who you can find around White Horse.

35. Parades You Cannot Miss

Plymouth is, overall, a very festive town. We all come together to celebrate different holidays and to commemorate major events. The parades have always been my favorite thing about living in Plymouth. There is no better way to get into the spirit of a holiday than a parade.

Many people know that the Macy's Thanksgiving Day Parade is the largest Thanksgiving Parade. It is even broadcasted on television. What many people do not know is that Plymouth has the second largest Thanksgiving Parade. We have floats and some balloons like the Macy's Parade, on a much smaller scale. What we have a lot of is music. Between marching bands, cover bands, and local artists, you cannot help but dance. Our Thanksgiving parade is generally led by Boston news anchors, who also judge each participant in the parade at the end of the route. Always bring blankets and handwarmers to these parades because you may be out in the cold for a bit. It is so much fun. Bring a non-perishable food item with you to donate at the end of the parade on what looks like The Polar Express.

Our other major parade is our Fourth of July parade. There is a full motorcade, music, and plenty of fun to be had. Plymouth does a lot for the Fourth, but this kicks off the day. If you have kids with you, there is a chance that candy will be thrown their way. There are a lot of historic reenactments during this parade, so prepare for loud noises from old-timey guns and cannons.

36. Quality Theatre Without Broadway Prices or Traffic

Plymouth is home to Priscilla Beach Theatre. This local theatre company puts on productions of big named shows while only charging about $30 per person. These shows frequently sell out, as the quality of the performance is unlike any other local theatre troupe that you have ever seen. All of this was started in 1936 and has only gotten better. Part of the charm? The theatre is an old barn!

Priscilla Beach Theatre has taken on shows like *Little Shop of Horrors*, *Grease,* and several other big names. Not only have the shows been big names, but some of the Priscilla Beach Theatre company members have turned into big stars. Included in this list are: Paul Newman, Peter Gallagher, and Jennifer Coolidge. Most of these notable people have thanked Priscilla Beach Theatre for inspiring them or helping them along the way. Priscilla Beach Theatre also offers workshops for aspiring performers.

If you would like to attend a show, check out the PBT website to see what shows will be playing while you are in town. Buy your ticket the second you decide to go!

37. Colony Place is Your Shopping Destination

Colony Place is an outdoor shopping center located by the Kingston line. This is Plymouth's premier shopping destination. It is also where most of our chain restaurant locations are located within the town. Prior to this development, the number one shopping destination for Plymouth residents tended to be out of town!

There is a great variety of stores in this open-air mall. From shoe stores to clothing stores, and even grocery stores, it is ultimately one-stop shopping when you visit Colony Place. With all of the stores here, and the amount of land covered, you may want to make a day out of visiting here. There are also events that occur sporadically through the year within the shopping center. While it is harder to shop outdoors when it is cold out, the beautiful décor for the winter holiday season makes everything a little more magical and bearable.

Good news for our tourist friends, if you are here during the week, you can visit management during business hours to get a free coupon book. If that is not incentive to shop, I do not know what is!

38. Check Out Our Baseball Team

When you think of Boston, what do you think of? Most people will say the Red Sox. Boston teams tend to face a lot of scrutiny from those that do not live locally. The perfect solution to fulfill your sport-loving needs? A Plymouth based baseball team! What more of a fitting name than the Plymouth Pilgrims!

The Plymouth Pilgrims consists of the best-of-the-best in terms of college baseball players. Every summer, these players come from all over the country, stay with Plymouth residents, and represent Plymouth in the New England Collegiate Baseball League. This is a legitimate league that is sponsored by Major League Baseball. In other words, these players are fantastic!

Home games are currently played at Forges Field. Our mascot is turkey that you have to get a picture with before you leave. Help us cheer on our team. You never know, you

93

may see them in the MLB one day!

39. Indulge in the Town Rivalry- North Versus South

As briefly mentioned earlier, there is an intense rivalry between Plymouth North and Plymouth South High School. This rivalry really comes out in sports and can even start in middle school. This rivalry started in the 1980's when Plymouth South High School was initially built. The rest is history.

While you can go to any game that is North versus South and experience the intensity, nothing will beat the Thanksgiving game. This is when all of the alumni come out to watch and support their teams and even their children. This rivalry is so significant that radios stations and news stations alike report on the games between these teams. In the end, it is all in good fun.

As a tourist, here is how you can pick what team to

support. Would you rather be an eagle or a panther? If you

answered eagle, support Plymouth North, and Plymouth

south for the latter. Not enough to convince you? Let us

discuss school colors. Would you rather wear teal and black

or blue and white? Teal and black goes to South and blue and

white goes to North. No matter which way it goes, go

Plymouth!

40. Runners, Here Is Where To Go

We have a lot of runners in Plymouth that are dedicated to sticking to a schedule and training for races. Massachusetts does host quite a few well-known races and marathons through the year. If you are familiar with Plymouth, you may feel comfortable running the main roads. I would never recommend doing this, no matter how familiar you were with the roads, as there are a lot of swerves and hills, as well as roads that narrow without notice.

Myles Standish State Forest is one of the most common places for people to train and race. The roads are not as popular as some of our main roads, making it a little safer to run up and down. There are some hills and swerves to help prepare you for if you are running a local race soon, but nothing like the main road. You can start slow.

If you need to train on bumpy terrain, you can use the walk paths. Always run with someone through the state forest, especially if you are not familiar with it. This can help

so you do not get lost and is an overall rule of thumb.

Running through the state forest is its own adventure. Make a

day of it so you can explore all of the different roads and

paths within it.

"In my opinion, this is the best Thanksgiving Parade in the nation. Every year has a well-planned theme, and everything lines up with it."

-David Jehle via America's Hometown Thanksgiving Testimonials

Samantha Anderson

100

41. Top Tourist Times

Living in a tourist town, you start gauging when tourists come the most, how long they stay, and when they start learning the insider tricks. Most of this is because you have to plan your commute to work, but there are just some parts of the year you do not have to worry about it.

Summer is an incredibly busy tourist time for us. Since we are so close to Cape Cod, we are a common stop when people are heading to the Cape, although we are a destination as well. The kids are out of school, there are a lot of activities for families, and we get put on a lot of bucket lists which makes times particularly crazy for us. Add Plymouth traffic in with Cape traffic and it is almost impossible to use the highway around the weekend. This normally kicks off around Memorial Day and does not end until Labor Day. If you are traveling during these months, it could take you over 3 hours, if not more, to get from Plymouth to over the bridge.

101

Our other popular tourist time is November. Since we are the home of the Pilgrims and the First Thanksgiving, people like to come here to feel like they get to experience a piece of this. With our parade also luring people in, we experience a huge surge of people during the month. The day of the parade is intense downtown, since there are activities after the parade as well. The busy times are worth it in the end, no matter how long we all sit in traffic.

42. There Is No Such Thing As Free Parking

My dear sweet tourists… nothing in this life truly comes for free. To park in downtown Plymouth, you are going to have to pay. Park Plymouth is very strict about paying to park. If you even think your time is running low in your meter, go add some more money. If not, you will end up with a ticket. The day of my wedding, we received a ticket because there were five minutes until the "free" parking started when our meter time ended.

Do not fret tourists, it is not just you that has to pay. Residents of Plymouth have to pay to park as well, even if they are parking for work. It is a huge controversy within the town. At least we know there is some guaranteed revenue!

I exaggerated a bit in the beginning. There are times during the year when parking is free. These are usually during our off months and it all kicks up again in summer. During the months when you have to pay to park, there are

103

times that you do not have to pay. It tends to be during the night. Always be sure to read the parking rules closely. No one will be spared. Also, parking lots by the waterfront fill up quickly. Take public transportation or shuttles whenever possible to save yourself the frustration of finding a spot and chancing a ticket.

43. Watch Out for the Rotary

Roundabouts, traffic circles, rotaries, or whatever else you want to call them, they are a tourist season's worst nightmare. Massachusetts has some doozies in terms of rotaries that cause miles and miles of traffic backups.

Downtown Plymouth has a small rotary along the waterfront. When they were redesigning the rotary, they made it way too small to the point that they had to redesign it because firetrucks could not fit through. Overall, it is still poorly designed. People can enter and exit from four different locations. The diameter is still so small that it is difficult for larger vehicles to go through. If you are renting a car, be aware that you may have to get it around a tiny rotary.

A friendly reminder that, in Massachusetts, the driver that is already in the rotary has the right of way. Everyone else must yield. Rotaries, especially ones that are so small, can cause accidents. Always be aware of your surroundings.

105

A bonus fact that makes this rotary awful: there is a

crosswalk in the middle of it.

44. A Thanksgiving Fit For Pilgrims

With the First Thanksgiving happening in this very town, it is no wonder that we do everything so dramatically. From our reenactments, to all our historic buildings, we take passion in our history.

What could be more historic and a better tribute to our ancestors than a reenactment of the First Thanksgiving? On Thanksgiving, Plimoth Plantation offers a Thanksgiving Day of some of the most notable Thanksgiving foods. There is traditional décor, fresh food, and history. You have to buy tickets for Thanksgiving at Plimoth Plantation in advance.

There are two different programs: The Thanksgiving Day Homestyle Buffet or the "Story of Thanksgiving" Dinner. The buffet is exactly that, a buffet. The Story of Thanksgiving features dinner and an interactive show- role players act as the Pilgrims and Wampanoag during the First Thanksgiving. Good food and entertainment!

107

45. Christmas in Plymouth

If you have not gotten the sense that Plymouth does the holidays in spectacular fashion, you will with Christmas. Christmas in Plymouth is filled with activities, performances, and absolute beauty. We start the holiday season when December begins with our annual Christmas tree lighting. Every year, Plymouth finds a spectacular tree to transplant into the center of town. In recent years, they have asked local businesses to create giant ornaments for the tree, which is also decorated with lights. The town comes together to celebrate the first lighting of the Christmas tree. There are carolers, dancers, and even an appearance from Santa himself that night!

Through the month, there are performances and activities to celebrate all of the winter holidays at Plymouth Memorial Hall and other great destinations in Plymouth. Some of these events are exclusively for kids, some are exclusively for adults, and others are for the family. There are performances from the Plymouth Philharmonic as well as local dance studios and bands to help everyone get cheery and bright.

No matter where you go downtown, all of the locations can take your breath away at night time with the lights. When the snow first falls, the lights become even more beautiful. If that happens while you are here, go walking downtown to see all of the lights. You will not regret it.

46. A Fourth of July Spectacular

I touched on the patriotism of Plymouth earlier when I wrote about the Fourth of July parade. The parade just kicks off the holiday with a bang, but Plymouth turns red, white, and blue for the day. It is an incredible phenomenon to witness.

Through the day on the Fourth of July, there are bands playing through the day. They play Memorial Hall, the pavilion by Brewster Gardens, and some local restaurants. What is so patriotic about these bands? In most cases, these are instrumental/marching bands that are all veterans or active military members. They come together to celebrate America with us. These bands come from all over the country to perform for a day in Plymouth.

At the end of the day, once the festivities have slowed down a bit, there is a surge of people in downtown Plymouth. This is for the yearly fireworks display. A large barge goes into Plymouth Harbor to set off fireworks that you can see from anywhere along the waterfront. Depending on where you sit, some locations will be playing patriotic music. My favorite part of our fireworks display was always trying to find the new shapes (i.e. smiley faces, thumbs up, or hearts). What firework will you see that is unique?

47. Head to the Green in Any Section of Plymouth

Golfers, Plymouth is your paradise. Every part of Plymouth has at least one golf course. There is a significant amount of golf courses spread out throughout the town. If you are looking to practice your swing on vacation, you have surely booked a hole in one by staying here.

One of the most popular golf courses is at White Cliffs. White Cliffs is in Cedarville, a village of Plymouth. This area is an exclusive community, with fabulous condos throughout. The golf course can be seen from the roadway and is always very well maintained. Another golf course that is close to this one is at Atlantic Country Club. This one is a little more hidden from the public and requires a drive down very narrow roads, but it is worth it.

An exit up has Waverly Oaks Golf Club, Crosswinds

Golf Club, and even Pinehills Golf Club. Pinehills has particularly good food in their clubhouse, which is a satellite location for East Bay Grille. There are so many other golf courses in Plymouth that you will have to do your research to see which one best suits you. You can always visit more than one. Expect great service from each of these courses as well as beautiful greens.

48. Give Yourself a Spa Day; Splurge, or Go with a Budget

Plymouth has a fantastic array of spas throughout the town. The most talked about spas are Mirabeau and Aristocracy. They are luxurious spas that offer full services. Mirabeau is exclusively a spa that offers massages, facials, and nail services among other services. Aristocracy is a hair salon that also offers great spa services, with their facials and nail services being their main highlights. A downside to Aristocracy is that there is no elevator and all of their spa services are on the second floor. These spas are a bit expensive, but the quality of the services is well worth the money.

If you are looking for a cheaper alternative, Plymouth has several nail and hair salons through the town. UV Nails is very accommodating for large groups and even kids. There is also Hollywood Nails that has always been a great place to go. These nail salons can be your mini-spa day, just to get away and do something for yourself for a moment. You deserve it!

49. Walk the Jetty to Blend in with Locals

Over the years, when people have not had anything to do, they have always said: "Let's go walk the jetty." The jetty is in downtown Plymouth and extends out into Plymouth Harbor. It is a popular place!

The jetty is approximately a mile long, give or take a bit. It makes my heart race a bit, especially seeing kids out there. There is not much protection as you walk further onto the jetty. It starts off with some hand rails, but then you are on your own. Be advised that on windy or rainy days, it can become even more dangerous.

However, if you are brave enough to walk the jetty, you will get some gorgeous ocean views. It is great for taking pictures, walking off dinner, or just to get a little bit of a rush. While the jetty can be very romantic, this is not an ideal proposal spot. There are too many ways that a ring could fall through the rocks or just straight into the ocean. Just enjoy the views with whoever you are traveling with.

50. Explore

The best way to experience Plymouth as though you live here is to explore all of these places, but then explore on your own as well. You never know what you can stumble upon. There are plenty of historic houses, monuments, and other hidden gems within the town.

Once you get to your destination (i.e. downtown, exit 7, or wherever) walk around and talk to locals, even if these locals are ones that are working our shops and restaurants. Everyone experiences Plymouth a little differently. Getting other takes on what you should do never hurts. While all of the major Plymouth related events and landmarks are in this book, there may be something that pertains to your personal interest niche that your waitress may know more about.

No matter how you spin it, you are going to have so much fun in Plymouth. There is too much to do and too much to enjoy to not have fun. Embrace the moments and take

pictures, but once in a while, put your phone away and just

take it all in.

Top Reasons to Book This Trip

- **History**: We have a rich historic background with the resources to educate you in an enjoyable manor.

- **Family Fun**: There are endless activities for all of the members of your family.

- **Food**: With endless amounts of locally owned restaurants that serve up fresh seafood and other entrees, our food is like no other.

Samantha Anderson

> TOURIST

GREATER THAN A TOURIST

Visit GreaterThanATourist.com
http://GreaterThanATourist.com

Sign up for the Greater Than a Tourist Newsletter
http://eepurl.com/cxspyf

Follow us on Facebook:
https://www.facebook.com/GreaterThanATourist

Follow us on Pinterest:
http://pinterest.com/GreaterThanATourist

Follow us on Instagram:
http://Instagram.com/GreaterThanATourist

Samantha Anderson

> TOURIST

GREATER THAN A TOURIST

Please leave your honest review of this book on Amazon and Goodreads. Thank you.

We appreciate your positive and negative feedback as we try to provide tourist guidance in their next trip from a local.

Our Story

Traveling is a passion of the "Greater than a Tourist" series creator. Lisa studied abroad in college, and for their honeymoon Lisa and her husband toured Europe. During her travels to Malta, an older man tried to give her some advice based on his own experience living on the island since he was a young boy. She was not sure if she should talk to the stranger but was interested in his advice. When traveling to some places she was wary to talk to locals because she was afraid that they weren't being genuine. Through her travels, Lisa learned how much locals had to share with tourists. Lisa created the "Greater Than a Tourist" book series to help connect people with locals. A topic that locals are very passionate about sharing.

Samantha Anderson

Notes

All experiences in this book are based on the author's personal opinions and experiences, as well as some excellent word-of-mouth.

Printed in Great Britain
by Amazon

24956183R00078